AT HOME IN WORLD WAR TWO

WOMEN'S WAR

Stewart Ross

IMPERIAL WAR
MUSEUM

Evans

Evans Brothers Limited

Published by Evans Brothers Limited
2A Portman Mansions
Chiltern Street
London W1U 6NR

© White-Thomson Publishing Limited 2002

Produced for Evans Brothers Limited by
White-Thomson Publishing Ltd
2/3 St Andrew's Place
Lewes, East Sussex BN7 1UP

Printed in Dubai

Editor: Philippa Smith
Consultant: Terry Charman, Historian, Research and Information Department,
Imperial War Museum
Designer: Christopher Halls, Mind's Eye Design, Lewes
Proofreader: Alison Cooper

British Library Cataloguing in Publication Data
Ross, Stewart
    Women's War. - (At home in World War Two)
    1. World War, 1939-1945 - Women - Great Britain
    I. Title
    941'.084'082
ISBN: 0 237 52305 1

Captions:
Cover and this page: A Government poster encouraging women to help with the war
effort by working in factories making armaments.
Cover (centre): Women engineers of the Women's Auxiliary Air Force (WAAF) working
on an aircraft engine. Before the war, this sort of work was done only by men.
Cover (background): Members of the Women's Land Army ploughing fields. Because of
the shortage of labour, the number of tractors in use on Britain's farms increased
dramatically during the war.
Title page: On His Majesty's Service (OHMS) – a group of Land Army women off to
work in the Devon countryside.
Contents page: Wrens testing a Lewis machine gun. Women were allowed to fire guns
in training and servicing centres, but not in action.

For sources of quoted material see page 31.

CONTENTS

TOTAL WAR

Britain joined World War Two in September 1939 when it declared war on Germany. France, Belgium, the Netherlands, Poland and other countries fought with Britain against Germany and, later, against Italy. In 1941, the USSR and the USA joined the war on the same side as Britain. Japan joined the side of Germany and Italy. This spread the fighting right round the world. The war finally ended in 1945.

Fighting in World War Two took place on land, at sea and in the air. Air raids by German bombers destroyed millions of homes and killed and injured thousands of people. Everyone's home might be in the 'front line'. That is why we say the war was fought on the 'Home Front' as well as the battle front.

▼ A mother and child, bombed out of their home in Coventry. Air raids meant that everyone, even women like this with young children to look after, was in the front line.

World War Two was a 'total' war. This means that the warring countries did everything they could to win. Every person, every factory and every field was needed for the war effort. Women's work was just as important as men's.

Before the war many British women, especially married and middle-class women, did not have paid jobs. The war changed this completely. Because millions of men were in the armed forces, women had to take over their jobs. Some of them did work women had never done before, such as driving tanks and building ships.

Women helped Britain to win the war. This book examines what they did and looks at how the war changed their lives.

THE PATH TO WAR

Adolf Hitler became leader of Germany in 1933. Backed by his Nazi Party, he removed those who were against him and began taking over neighbouring countries. After Germany took over Czechoslovakia, Britain and France promised other countries that they would oppose Nazi aggression if the Germans attacked anyone else. On 1 September 1939, Hitler invaded Poland. Two days later, Britain and France declared war on Germany.

▼ *Women of the ATS (Auxiliary Territorial Service) guiding the turret of a Churchill tank into position. Other women are working on the engine and the tracks.*

THE CALL UP

Diana Thomas, broadcasting on the BBC Home Service (now Radio 4) in May 1941, urged all women to volunteer to do war work:

> 'Today we are calling all women. Every woman in the country is needed to pull her weight to the utmost . . . It's no longer a question of what is the most comfortable arrangement for each family. We are fighting for our lives – for our freedom and our future. We are all in it together, and what is already being done by other women you can do. Don't be afraid of being alone in your sacrifice – however great it may be . . . All those little things that are so important in every woman's life – we treasure them and cling to them, they are our life-blood. And now we have got to fight for them. Isn't it worth it? Together, yes it is.'

▼ A collection of posters urging women to join the armed forces or sign up for voluntary work. The images make the work look much more exciting than it usually was.

At the time Diana Thomas made her appeal, the country was desperately short of workers. At the beginning of the war, all men between the ages of 18 and 41 had to prepare for conscription (joining the forces or doing other war work). Women were not conscripted because the Government, including the Prime Minister, Winston Churchill, believed it would damage family life.

By 1941, although many women had volunteered for work, many more were needed. So in April 1941, the Government said women would be called up (conscripted). Britain was the first country ever to do this.

'I went to Colwyn Bay and volunteered for the forces. I was about 18 or 19. After passing our flying flea inspection, as we called the medical, I was accepted into the WAAF. I don't know why the WAAF – I just fancied it.'

Ann Fox

◀ So you want to join up, do you? A new recruit (left) is interviewed by an ATS corporal. A range of ATS posters is displayed on the wall behind them.

At first, only single women under 26 were conscripted. Later, women aged between 18 and 51 had to register to do war work. There were exceptions, however – women with children under the age of 14 had the choice whether or not to take on this work.

◀ Mrs Dart, of Bristol, with the five children she looked after while their mothers were at work. Nurseries and child-minders were vital if women were to take part in war work.

LEFT, RIGHT!

In 1938, when war looked likely, the army wanted as many recruits as possible. The Government set up a women's branch of the army known as the ATS (Auxiliary Territorial Service). Within a year the ATS had 17,000 women volunteers, and by 1943 its numbers had grown to more than 200,000.

ATS recruits wore black shoes (not army boots) and khaki uniforms – even their underwear was khaki! Like regular soldiers, they lived in barracks and learned to march, salute and obey orders. In December 1941 they became an equal part of Britain's armed forces. Male and female soldiers were paid the same: two shillings (about 10p) a day plus food and accommodation. Some men were annoyed at having to salute female ATS officers, but they changed their attitude when they saw what good soldiers the women were.

Women were not allowed to fire guns or go into action. Apart from this, they did the same work as men in Britain and overseas. Because the army was rather old-fashioned, many women were given safe jobs as cooks, clerks and telephonists. Others worked as lorry drivers, motorbike riders, engineers and translators.

JOIN THE ATS

ASK FOR INFORMATION AT THE NEAREST EMPLOYMENT EXCHANGE OR AT ANY ARMY OR ATS RECRUITING CENTRE

▲ This ATS recruiting poster suggests that joining up is glamorous. This was done because the army had a reputation for being rather dowdy and unfeminine.

▶ West Indian recruits to the ATS wait to be taken to training camp. Once there, their smart clothes and jewellery will disappear into a bottom drawer.

'I drove a three-ton truck. It was lovely living all that way from home.'

ATS member Mary Beck

◀ *An ATS anti-aircraft crew in west London, 1941. They are acting as 'spotters' – looking out for enemy aircraft.*

Perhaps the ATS's most important work was in Anti-Aircraft Command. This found, tracked and shot down enemy aircraft with anti-aircraft guns. Women operated the radar and searchlights and aimed the guns – but only men were allowed to fire them.

In 1940 a survey found that the great majority of women thought it was fair that they should be conscripted alongside the men. These words from an advertisement for Yardley cosmetics, which also appeared in 1940, reflected this mood:

'We asked for equal rights and we cannot have it both ways. It is only fair that we should face the music side by side with our men.'

▶ *Princess Elizabeth (now Queen Elizabeth II) explains to her mother the work she is doing as an ATS mechanic. The Princess joined the ATS because she wished people to see the Royal Family working for victory alongside everyone else.*

By Air and Sea

WAAF recruits learn to handle a heavy barrage balloon. At the start of the war, the RAF said women would not be able to manage tough jobs like this. They were proved wrong!

Women served with the Royal Air Force in the WAAF (Women's Auxiliary Air Force) and with the Royal Navy in the WRNS (Women's Royal Naval Service). By late 1943 there were about 182,000 women in the WAAF and 74,000 in the WRNS. Their blue uniforms were smarter than those of the ATS and from 1941 many WAAFs wore trousers for work.

Like the ATS, women in the WAAF were not allowed to fight. They did, however, work in areas targeted by enemy bombers. During the Battle of Britain (July–October 1940), for example, women operated key radar positions that warned of approaching enemy aircraft. By 1943, 22 per cent of air force personnel on airfields were women. By the end of the war 70 per cent of the WAAF did skilled work, such as engineering.

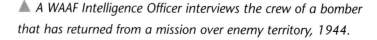

▲ *A WAAF Intelligence Officer interviews the crew of a bomber that has returned from a mission over enemy territory, 1944.*

Women were vital to the Air Transport Auxiliary (ATA) which flew aircraft from factories to airfields and between airfields. Over half the ATA personnel were women. Female pilots flew all kinds of planes, from fighters to heavy bombers. During the war 12 women ATA pilots were killed in crashes.

WRNS members (known as 'Wrens') were not allowed to go to sea on fighting warships and, unlike the ATS and WAAF, they did not have the same pay and status as men. Even so, some had important and difficult jobs. They worked as drivers, engineers, radar operators and in meteorology (weather forecasting). Boat's Crew Wrens, like Rozelle Raynes (see below), operated powerful harbour launches.

▲ Ready for take-off. A Wren radio mechanic prepares to flight test the equipment on which she has been working.

◀ Wrens wheel a torpedo towards a submarine, ready for loading. Women doing work ashore freed more men to serve on ships, which had all-male crews.

In 1944, Rozelle Raynes commanded the cutter HMS *Squid*. One stormy night she was ordered to collect some soldiers from a landing craft anchored at sea:

> 'It was a pitch black night with the wind screaming in the rigging like a thousand demented demons. Enormous white-crested waves reared up out of the blackness . . . the sailors [we were collecting] jumped on to the rope ladder with the speed of grasshoppers and the last thing we heard . . . was the voice of the Belgian skipper . . . shouting into the gale: "Nom d'une sacrée vache! Ce sont des femmes là-bas, dans ce bateau!"' [Holy cow! They are women down there in that boat!]

11

'I LEARNED TO PLOUGH'

Kathleen Hale was an art student when war broke out. Because she loved horses, she joined an organisation of female farm workers known as the Women's Land Army:

'I learned to plough. When I was told to plough, first I thought, what on earth do I do? Then I remembered somebody saying that if you can see the trace of the previous furrow go straight beside that and you will be all right. So I did, but it was a very old-fashioned, heavy wooden plough, which all the people on the farm called the 'man-killer'. I soon learned why when it turned and knocked me over at each turn. I was terrified the other workers would see me, so I scrambled to my feet and continued. This went on all the time, and in the end I couldn't use it.

The Land Army supplied an awful uniform . . . A sort of khaki overall and puttees, a word which nowadays nobody understands. [Puttees are a sort of legging.] And we had a badge, and some awful kind of felt hat with no shape.'

▼ This Women's Land Army recruitment poster gives an unrealistic idea of Land Army life. In reality, work with the Land Army was usually extremely tough.

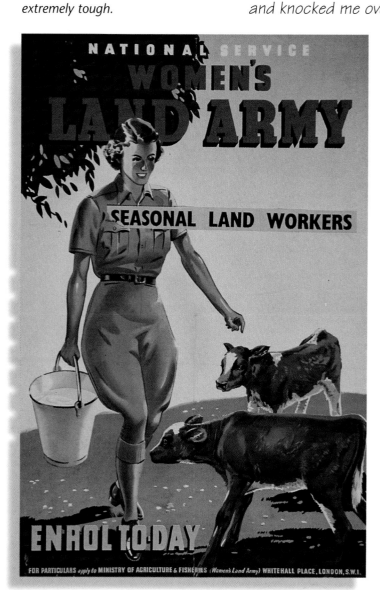

▼ The ploughgirl replaced the ploughboy on many farms – and earned lower wages, too.

As importing food was dangerous and expensive, Britain needed as much home-grown food as possible. In June 1939 the Women's Land Army was formed to work in the countryside. It had 80,300 members by December 1943.

Land Army girls like Kathleen Hale earned one pound eight shillings a week (about £1.40), a lot less than male farm workers. Despite their 'awful' uniforms, difficult work and poor accommodation, they did a remarkable job: between 1939 and 1945 the proportion of Britain's food that was imported fell from two-thirds to one-third.

The Women's Land Army Song

Back to the land, with its clay and sand,
Its granite and gravel and grit,
You grow barley and wheat
And potatoes to eat
To make sure that the nation keeps fit.

▲ Land Army girls reaping wheat on the Sussex Downs, August 1941.

◄ Members of the Land Army Timber Corps loading pit props (used to support the tunnels in coal mines) that they have finished cutting. By 1943 Britain imported only 25 per cent of its timber, compared to 90 per cent before the war.

'NEVER SAY NO'

Not all women were free to do full-time work. Some had young children to look after, while others were too old or had to stay at home to look after families and relatives. Huge numbers of these women did their bit for the war effort through voluntary work.

Several groups organised women's voluntary work. These included Women's Institutes, whose work ranged from jam-making to collecting scrap metal, and the British Red Cross Society, which specialised in first aid and medical skills. The largest wartime women's organisation was the Women's Voluntary Service (WVS), set up in 1938. By 1944 one million members wore its uniform of school-style hats, and grey-green skirts and jackets.

If *you* can't go to the factory help the neighbour who *can*

How you can help

Arrange now with a neighbour to look after her children when she goes to her war-work—or give your name to

CARING FOR WAR WORKERS' CHILDREN IS A NATIONAL SERVICE

Issued by the Ministry of Health   MH 17

▲ *Everything that helped with the war effort was seen as a national service, as this poster shows. Before the war, most women with school-age children did not go out to work.*

▶ *Members of a Women's Institute using equipment sent from the USA to can locally-grown fruit.*

The WVS's watchword was 'never say no': it tried to do anything asked of it. It was founded to help during and after air raids. Until 1942 this work, led by the 200,000 members of its Housewife Section, took up much of its time. It ran canteens and rest centres for the homeless, organised evacuation, managed air-raid shelters and set up first-aid posts. It even established a Village Bicycle Shuttle Messenger Service to carry messages in an emergency.

▲ Mobile canteens run by the WVS were a welcome sight after an air raid. The women who staffed them were not paid.

'Bombs fell about 13.00. Head housewife and messenger on duty 13.04. C. Road housewives ready to help 13.05.

'Head housewife and messenger ran to damaged houses in C. Road and V. Road. Helped to rescue 13 children; packed them, rolled in blankets, into RAF lorry with housewife L. and daughter in charge. Sent them off to hospital.'

From the report of a Women's Voluntary Service head housewife, 1943

Later, the WVS branched out into other work, including unloading ships and running National Day Nurseries. These were places where working mothers could safely leave their children for one shilling (5p) a day. This important wartime idea led to the network of crèches and nurseries we have today.

Not all women entered into the helpful wartime spirit. The *News Chronicle* reported how a Mrs Bomzer of London broke two regulations: (1) selling eggs for more than their fixed price; (2) not informing her customers about her prices and goods.

'Fines and costs totalling £129 were imposed at Old Street yesterday on Mrs J Bomzer . . . on two summonses alleging overcharging for eggs and for failing to display notices and categories of eggs.'

28 May 1941

▲ A Home Guard instructor teaches a member of the Watford Women's Home Defence Unit how to fire a rifle. Only if the enemy had invaded would women have been allowed to fire guns in action.

MEN'S WORK, MEN'S PAY?

Although many women had jobs before the war, after 1939 the number of female workers more than doubled. This was to replace the men called up into the armed services, and to meet the pressing need for tanks, guns, aircraft and uniforms.

Thousands of women returned to jobs they had done before they married, like teaching and nursing. Others became bricklayers, bus conductresses and railway workers, and took on other jobs more usually done by men.

Registered women workers were divided into 'mobile' and 'immobile'. The 'mobile', usually quite young, had no family commitments and could be sent to work anywhere. Many ended up in new factories far from home and were housed in hostels. The 'immobile' were given work near their homes.

▲ *A group of women painters on their way to work on houses built for workers in an armaments factory.*

▶ *As skilled as any man – Sadie Nairn, an expert welder, at work on a minesweeper.*

Women factory workers often found themselves doing heavy jobs, such as welding and working lathes. Willing and just as skilful as men, they worked up to 60 hours a week or more. Thanks to their remarkable efforts Britain's output of war materials rose more quickly than anyone expected.

Most women didn't mind doing tough and difficult jobs. But they did mind being paid less than men for the same work. In one Glasgow factory skilled women machine operators received less than the man who cleaned the lavatories. In 1943 they went on strike. The employers accepted their argument and raised their pay. But they still earned less than men who did the same job.

A man visiting a factory making shells was surprised to find almost all the work being done by women:

> 'Hundreds of other machines in the shell shops around are doing . . . [other complicated] operations . . . At almost every stage women operators do the work . . . The women handle machines of all kinds, from the most powerful to the most delicate, in these complex processes. Even the huge portable cranes moving high overhead are manned by girls.'

▲ Taking over from the men. A woman is shown how to operate the machinery that makes hand-held machine guns. Although she would do a man's job, she would not receive a man's wages.

'The pay was unfair, I suppose, but we didn't mind because we were doing our bit for the war.'

Maureen Wint, who worked as a clerk in Dover docks

◀ Women working in a shipyard. Because hundreds of ships were sunk by enemy raiders, building new ships was absolutely vital war work.

NURSES AND FIRST-AIDERS

Diana Hutchinson wanted to be an army nurse. She joined the Red Cross in 1942, did three months' nurse's training, and was called up into the VAD (Voluntary Aid Department). Shortly afterwards she was working as a night nurse in a hospital in East Grinstead:

'I was on duty from eight o'clock until eight the next morning. It was very hard staying awake all night, even if you had slept in the day. Four o'clock in the morning was the worst time, and if Sister came round and found you asleep she rapped you on the knuckles. We had very little time off. I think it was three months on, one night off per week, and then three days off at the end of the three months. Otherwise we were on duty all the time.

▼ *The only survivors. A nurse cares for Sally (left) and Barbara Smith after an air raid, March 1941. The little girls' parents and brother were killed when a bomb fell on their house.*

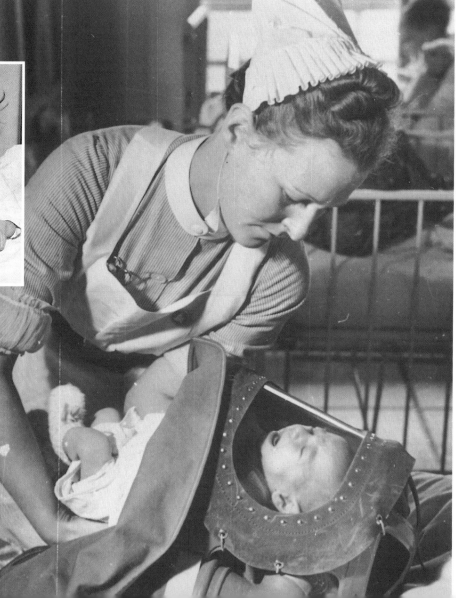

▶ *A nurse fits a new-born baby into a specially-made gas suit. Adults carried gas masks in case of poison gas attacks. Those too small to wear a mask had to be put in suits like these.*

I probably went home, but I can't remember how often. The trains were terribly cold. There was no loo paper, or soap or anything, no refreshments, no heating on the trains. But I enjoyed it all.'

Digging for victory. Nurses, and soldiers recovering from wounds, working together on the vegetable plot of a Bristol hospital, 1940.

There were plenty of nurses in 1939 because medicine was then one of the few professions open to women. Even so, more were needed. Like Diana Hutchinson, they were rushed through short training courses and sent straight to work. Only a handful of women trained as doctors.

In total, 343,100 women served as nurses and first-aiders with the Red Cross, St John's Ambulance, Auxiliary Nursing Service or Emergency Medical Service. They mostly remained in hospitals, although army nurses worked on the battlefield or brought injured soldiers home in air ambulances.

'EVERY NIGHT SOMETHING AWFUL!'

To us, life in wartime Britain seems dreadful: six years short of food, fuel and heating; in constant danger; losing friends and loved ones; doing without luxuries; dressed in drab clothes; often overworked and underpaid. Surprisingly, most British people remained cheerful and hopeful throughout the war. In other words, their morale was high.

▼ *A poster advertising ENSA's 'munition concerts', arranged specially for workers in the vital munitions industry.*

The nation's morale was its mood. Victory depended on it. If morale had collapsed in 1940, for example, the country might well have surrendered. The Government hoped to boost morale with rousing speeches, optimistic announcements and posters. It also spent £14 million on the Entertainments National Service Association (ENSA, which the comedian Tommy Trinder said stood for 'Every Night Something Awful'!).

ENSA's job was to boost civilian and military morale through entertainment. Four-fifths of singers, dancers, musicians, actors and actresses belonged to ENSA, earning a maximum of £10 a week. They broadcast on the BBC's 'Home Service' and 'Forces Programme' (the only radio stations) and gave two-and-a-half million live performances, at the rate of 5,000 a week, in factories and halls throughout the land and overseas. Not all of them, as Tommy Trinder noted, were of a very high standard.

Women were a vital part of ENSA. Singers like Gracie Fields, Anne Shelton (known as 'the forces' favourite') and Vera Lynn ('the forces' sweetheart') stirred their listeners' hearts with memories and dreams of a better world. Interestingly, the most popular song with soldiers on both sides was the German 'Lilli Marlene'.

Hans Leip wrote the lyrics of 'Lilli Marlene' in 1915. They were set to music in 1938, and in 1941 the song became popular with German soldiers. The British soon picked it up and Anne Shelton recorded a hit version with these English words written by Tommie Connor:

Underneath the lantern,
By the barrack gate,
Darling, I remember
The way you used to wait.
'Twas there that you whispered tenderly,
That you love me,
You'd always be
My Lilli of the Lamplight,
My own Lilli Marlene.

▼ *ENSA sing-songs were a cheap and easy way of keeping up the morale of men and women in the armed forces.*

▼ *Vera Lynn (centre), known as 'the forces' sweetheart', with a crowd of admiring factory workers.*

▲ *Any platform will do! The singer Gracie Fields climbs down a stairway of ammunition boxes from a makeshift stage. She has just finished an ENSA concert in an armaments factory.*

FRIENDS AND FAMILIES

The war gave women more freedom. Working away from home, they escaped the watchful eyes of their families. Responsibility increased their self-confidence. Although generally paid less than men, women still earned more than in peacetime. With their own money, they had more control over their lives.

It was a very emotional time, especially for those in the armed forces. Believing they would not live long, lots of couples rushed into marriage in 1939–40. The war put a huge strain on these and other relationships. Each time the couples met they knew it might be the last. Many spent months, or even years, apart.

As thousands of men were killed and relationships broke up under the strain of war, the number of one-parent families grew. Of the 4,655,000 children born between 1940 and 1945, 305,000 were born to single mothers. Life was particularly hard for unmarried mothers, who received no Government financial support.

▼ *Daddy's home! Lance Bombardier Jack Grundy, from the 8th Army, arrives home on leave, 1944.*

► *The letter no woman wanted to receive. The message stamp reads, 'It is regretted that this item could not be delivered because the addressee is reported prisoner of war.' Most men captured did not return home until the end of the war.*

By 1944 almost 1.5 million servicemen from the USA, Canada and other allied countries were stationed in Britain. The Americans (called 'GIs' because their clothes and equipment were marked 'Government Issue') were the most glamorous. They were well off (earning £3.44 a week compared with a British soldier's 70p), carefree and had plenty of rare luxuries, such as cigarettes and nylon stockings. Not surprisingly, many British girls went out with GIs. After the war 80,000 of them went to the USA as 'GI brides'.

▲ *Dancing with Yankees. ATS girls enjoying a night out with US soldiers based in Britain. After years of wartime hardship, British girls were attracted to the well-paid, cheerful American servicemen.*

'We thought the bombers were going to kill us all, so we married as soon as war broke out. Then my husband, who was in the RAF, was sent away and I went to work in Stoke Mandeville Hospital. We hardly saw each other for years. Then the Americans came – handsome and rich and kind – and, well, that was the end of my marriage.'

Marjorie Williams, a physiotherapist who married in 1939

◄ *British women, many with children, sail to join their American husbands (GIs) who have already returned to the USA.*

MAKING DO

Edith Carter, a housewife from Kent, married her husband in 1938. She recalls her life in Chatham during the war:

'Teddy, my husband, was in the Navy, so I didn't see much of him. I worried a lot – Where was he now? Was he OK? But most of the time I was too busy to think about anything else except looking after the children. Mary was born in 1939 and Robert in 1940, just after Dunkirk. It was very hard, lugging them off to the shelter when the sirens went, cluttered up with bottles and food and nappies and the gas masks . . . I didn't have much money but there wasn't much to spend it on. Everything was 'on rations', and even those things you couldn't get all the time. Shopping was a nightmare sometimes. I remember queuing for an hour once just to get bread. But at least I didn't have to worry about the kids pestering me for sweets – there weren't any.'

▼ Not the ideal night out. Carrying their bedding, Londoners queue to enter an air-raid shelter at the start of the Blitz, September 1940.

▶ The cheerful spirit of the Blitz. Londoners in an air-raid shelter share a joke as they wait for their evening meal to cook on a camp stove.

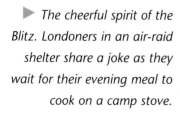

Edith Carter's experiences were shared by many women. The danger of bombing and the shortages of food and normal household goods, such as soap, made life very hard. And the more children a woman had, the tougher things became. The wife of an army private, for example, received an extra five shillings (25p) a week for the first child, three shillings (15p) for the second, two shillings (10p) for the third and one shilling (5p) for each child above that. The National Milk Scheme (1940) and Vitamin Welfare Scheme (1941) provided milk and vitamins at reduced prices.

Because of the shortages, women became expert at 'making do'. They learned to make clothes out of scraps of cloth, to paint their legs brown to look like stockings, and comb cats and dogs for 'wool' to spin into thread. To save sugar and fats, some women even decorated cakes with knitted 'icing'.

The punishment for wasting food was severe, as this newspaper report shows:

'Miss Mary Bridget O'Sullivan . . . was fined a total of ten pounds . . . for permitting bread to be wasted.'
Bristol Evening Post, 20 January 1943

▲ A mother and her daughter make wooden shutters to protect their windows against bomb blasts, September 1940. Shutters also acted as black-outs.

◄ Dress-making classes, Penzance, Cornwall. The models on the table are Lillian Serle (16) and Mrs Briggs, both evacuees from London. The shortage of material and ready-made clothes meant everyone had to learn to make and mend their own garments.

THE BRAVEST
OF THE BRAVE

Some women were engaged in top-secret war work. Before they started such employment they had to sign the Official Secrets Act, promising not to talk to anyone about what they were doing. Even when the war was over they were told to 'stay silent'. The most common type of secret work was with one of the Government ministries. A handful of women, mainly high-powered secretaries, worked in the Cabinet War Office, right at the heart of Government. It was based in an underground bunker off Whitehall in central London.

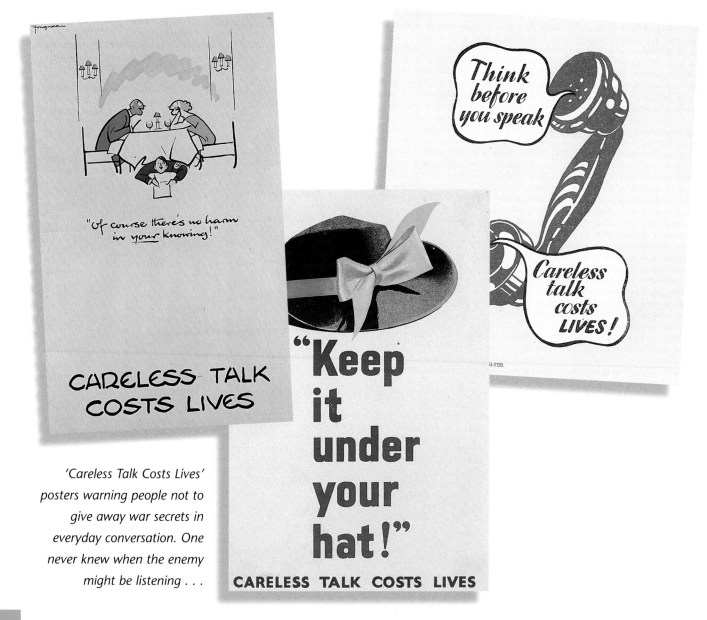

'Careless Talk Costs Lives' posters warning people not to give away war secrets in everyday conversation. One never knew when the enemy might be listening . . .

About 2,000 women, hand-picked for their intelligence and reliability, were employed at the Government Code and Cipher School at Bletchley Park, Buckinghamshire. Here, using an 'Enigma' machine (a kind of early computer), experts learned to read the Germans' top-secret coded messages. Because the Germans did not realise their messages were being intercepted, allied commanders learned of the enemy's plans in advance.

The First Aid Nursing Yeomanry (FANY), founded in 1907, was the oldest and most respected women's military force. In World War Two about 2,000 FANYs joined the secret Special Operations Executive (SOE). A handful of them, like Violette Szabo and Odette Hallowes (see below), were sent to work as agents in lands occupied by the enemy. Among the most remarkable was Captain Nancy Wake, who ended up commanding 7,000 French in the Auvergne district of France. These women, all of whom risked torture and execution, were the bravest of the brave.

▲ *Women operating the switchboard at the Ministry of Information. Note that the person in charge is a man – although the women were badly needed as workers, they were not often given positions of responsibility.*

In 1942 Odette Hallowes, a mother of three children, went to France as a secret agent. She was captured and tortured but, with incredible bravery, survived to tell her story:

> *'My children were my entire life . . . I don't think anybody realised that I was absolutely heartbroken the day I left . . . From the moment I arrived in France I was a French woman who had not left France at all. I was a widow. I had a new name, new identity and everything.'*

▲ *My daughter or my duty? Violette Szabo volunteered to work as a special agent in France only weeks after the birth of her daughter. Eventually, she was captured after a bitter gunfight, tortured and shot.*

◄ *The spy princess. Princess Noor Khan, whose father was an Indian prince and whose mother was an American, worked in France for British Intelligence under the code name Madelaine. In 1944 she was betrayed to the Germans and shot.*

NEW WOMEN

Every woman's experience of the war was different. Nevertheless, the years of conscription and voluntary work had dramatically changed millions of lives.

First, more women than ever had jobs and money of their own: in May 1945 there were 460,000 women in the armed services and more than 6.5 million in other war work. Moreover, from 1945, child benefit was paid directly to mothers. These developments increased women's independence and freedom.

Second, women had proved they could compete in a man's world. In almost every sphere – from drivers and steel workers to military officers and secret agents – they had performed at least as well as men. If they had done so during the war, why not in peacetime?

▲ At last! Londoner Pat Burgess whoops with delight at the news that the war is over. Her chief hope now is that her husband will return home safely.

► A selection of newspaper headlines announcing the end of the war – VE stood for 'Victory in Europe'. Peace was as welcome as victory.

Third, women had learned to manage at home on their own. When the men came home they were surprised, and sometimes distressed, to find they were no longer 'the master'. This strained many relationships. There were twice as many divorces in 1945 as in 1930.

Peace temporarily reversed many of the wartime changes. Perhaps surprisingly, in 1945, 75 per cent of working women said they wanted to become traditional housewives. This is often what happened. The women's armed forces were run down and returning men took over many of the jobs women had been doing.

Even before the war ended, some women realised what was likely to happen:

> 'I don't think things look too good for after the war. A lot of girls would like to stay on, and the boys will come back and want the jobs.'

Remark made to Mass Observation (an organisation that kept a detailed record of how people lived) in 1944

In September 1944 the *Daily Mirror* reported the Government's plans for releasing men and women from the armed forces (demobbing):

> 'Women will be demobbed or transferred to reconstruction [rebuilding] like men, with this difference: married women will be treated as a priority class.'

Married women could be released early because it was assumed they would not want jobs. Nevertheless, the clock could not be put back. In the 1960s and 1970s, when their daughters began calling for equal rights for women, their mothers understood what they were saying. They knew that women could share the world with men, not just help in a man's world.

▲ Two sailors and their girlfriends celebrate VE day with a dip in the fountains of London's Trafalgar Square.

▼ Women from the Office of War Information dance in the streets of London on VE day, 1945. For a few brief moments, people could forget the tremendous task of getting the country back to normal after more than five years of war.

GLOSSARY

air-raid shelter A place where people could shelter from a bomb attack. Many were underground.

allied countries The USA and other countries that fought against Germany, Italy and Japan.

armaments Weapons of war.

armed forces The army, navy and air force.

ATS The Auxiliary Territorial Service, the women's branch of the army.

barracks Accommodation for the armed forces.

black-outs Covers put over all windows at night so that no light showed outside. This was done to make it harder for enemy bombers to find target towns in the darkness.

Blitz The heavy bombing of a city. 'Blitz' comes from the German word *Blitzkrieg* which means 'lightning war'.

bunker A concrete and steel shelter, usually underground.

call up An expression that means the same as 'conscript'.

canteen A place where food and drink is served.

conscript To require someone to join the armed forces or do other war work.

cutter A small, fast ship.

Dunkirk A port in north-east France from which the defeated British army was brought home in 1940.

ENSA The Entertainments National Service Association. It employed entertainers to keep up people's morale.

evacuation Moving people to a safe place, usually out of towns and cities.

imported Brought in from other countries.

invaded Moved into another country by force.

landing craft A small, flat-bottomed boat used for landing troops on beaches.

lathe A machine for shaping wood or metal.

ministry A Government department, e.g. the Ministry of Food.

Nazi Party Germany's National Socialist Party. It was led by Adolf Hitler and followed his ideas and wishes.

personnel People employed in a business or in the armed forces.

radar A machine for detecting objects, such as aircraft, before they are close enough to be seen.

rationing Limiting the amount of food and certain other goods people were allowed to buy during the war. It made sure that everyone had an equal share of these items.

recruit Someone joining the armed forces.

shell A large bullet that explodes when it hits its target.

status One's position in society; how someone is regarded by other people.

translators People who change speech or writing from one language to another.

voluntary Something one can choose to do – or not.

WAAF The Women's Auxiliary Air Force, the women's branch of the Royal Air Force.

WRNS The Women's Royal Naval Service, the women's branch of the Royal Navy.

WVS The Women's Voluntary Service, which organised a range of wartime services, from running mobile canteens to collecting scrap metal.

PROJECTS ON WOMEN IN WORLD WAR TWO

Interview two women who lived through World War Two. Ask them the same questions, then write out the questions with the different answers under each one. What are the similarities and differences?

Write an illustrated diary of a member of the Women's Land Army, using as much primary evidence as you can.

A project on this topic needs information from *primary* and *secondary* sources. Secondary sources, mainly books and websites, are listed on the next page. They give mostly other people's views about women's wartime experiences. Primary sources come from the time of the war, like some of the quotations in this book. They make a project really interesting and original.

Here are some ways of getting hold of primary information:

- Talking to women who lived through the war.
- Looking for objects remaining from the war. These can be large things like buildings. For example, is there an air-raid shelter still standing near you? Smaller objects include gas masks and ration books.
- Visiting museums. Most local museums have excellent displays about their area during World War Two. National museums, like the Imperial War Museum in London and Bletchley Park in Buckinghamshire, have a great deal of information.
- Looking at old photographs in family albums.
- Reading printed memories. There are many collections of old photographs, too. Ask at your local library what there is for your area.
- Visiting websites that contain primary information – but read the warning on the next page first!

FURTHER INFORMATION

BOOKS TO READ

All About the Second World War, Pam Robson (Hodder Wayland, 1996)
Britain Through the Ages: Britain Since 1930, Stewart Ross (Evans, 1995)
Coming Alive: Dear Mum, I Miss You! Stewart Ross (Evans, 2001)
Coming Alive: What If the Bomb Goes Off? Stewart Ross (Evans, 2001)
Family Life: Second World War, Nigel Smith (Hodder Wayland, 1998)
The History Detective Investigates Britain at War: Women's War, Martin Parsons (Hodder Wayland, 2000)
History in Writing: The Second World War, Christine Hatt (Evans, 2000)
In Grandma's Day: War, Faye Gardner (Evans, 2000)
Investigating the Home Front, Alison Honey (The National Trust, 1996)
Keep Smiling Through: Women in the Second World War, Caroline Lang (CUP, 1989)
The Little Ships, Louise Borden (Pavilion, 1997)

WEBSITES

Just because information is on the web, it does not mean it is true. Anyone can put anything they want on a website. Well-known organisations like the BBC, a university or the Imperial War Museum have sites you can trust. If you are unsure about a site, ask your teacher. Here are a few useful sites to start from (don't forget http:// or http://www.):

angelfire.com/la/raeder/England.html
bbc.co.uk/history/wwtwo.shtml
british-forces.com/world_war2
historyplace.com/worldwar2
iwm.org.uk/lambeth/lambeth.htm
members.tripod.com/~Gerry_Wiseman/feature_article.htm

Picture acknowledgements:
The following images courtesy of the Imperial War Museum. Figures following page numbers refer to photograph negative numbers:
Cover and imprint page poster: PST3645, cover (centre): CH10667, cover (background): HU36275, title page: D21958, contents page: A13209, p.4: HU36245, p.5: H24517, p.6 (left): PST5873, (centre): Art Dept poster, (right): 3096, p.7 (top): HU36278, (bottom): D10547, p.8 (top): Art Dept poster, (bottom): AP14372D, p.9 (top): H15452, (bottom): H41644, p.10 (top left): CH7346, (bottom): CH12687, p.11 (top right): A9115, (centre): A19470, p.12 (left): Art Dept poster, (bottom): HU63823, p.13 (top): HU36274, (bottom): HU63764, p.14 (top): 0773, (bottom): HU63761, p.15 (top): HU687, (bottom): HU36277, p.16 (top): P243, (bottom): A8989, p.17 (top): TR639, (bottom): HU36242, p.18 (left): HU36160, (right): D651, p.19: HU63750, p.20: PST3384, p.21 (top): P553, (bottom right): P76, p.22 (left): TR1643, (bottom): envelope courtesy of Mr A. J. Richardson, p.23 (top): HU55851, (bottom): HU36289, p.24 (left): HU36144, (bottom): D1604, p.25 (top): HU36139, (bottom): D2203, p.26 (left): PST0650, (centre): PST0164, (right): PST0731, p.27 (top): D5367, (lower right): HU16541, (bottom): HU28683, p.28 (left) FOX66398, (bottom): D24583, p.29 (top): EA65799, (bottom): EA65796.

Poster on p.21 courtesy of Robert Opie.

Sources of quoted material:
Page 6:   Taken from Caroline Lang, *Keep Smiling Through: Women in the Second World War*, CUP, Cambridge, 1989, p.31
Page 7:   Taken from Mavis Nicholson, ed., *What Did You Do in the War, Mummy?*, Chatto and Windus, London, 1995, p.77
Page 9 (top): Taken from Fiona Reynoldson, *Women's War*, Wayland Publishers Ltd., Hove, 1991, p.17
Page 11:   Taken from *The War Papers*, no.29, Peter Way and Marshall Cavendish Partworks Ltd., London, 1976
Page 12:   Taken from Mavis Nicholson, ed., *What Did You Do in the War, Mummy?*, Chatto and Windus, London, 1995, pp.121–2
Page 13:   Song taken from Caroline Lang, *Keep Smiling Through: Women in the Second World War*, CUP, Cambridge, 1989, p.32
Page 15:   WVS report taken from *Ourselves in Wartime*, Odhams, London, p.149
Page 17 (centre): Taken from *Ourselves in Wartime*, Odhams, London, p.18
Page 17 (right): Personal interview with author, 2000
Page 18–19: Taken from Mavis Nicholson, ed., *What Did You Do in the War, Mummy?* Chatto and Windus, London, 1995, pp.151–2
Page 21:   Tommie Connor's words taken from Robbie Rhodes, *The Saga of 'Lilli Marlene'*, MMD Archives
Pages 23 and 24: Personal interviews with author
Page 27:   Taken from Mavis Nicholson, ed., *What Did You Do in the War, Mummy?*, Chatto and Windus, London, 1995, p.239–40

INDEX

Numbers in **bold** refer to pictures and captions.